WELCOME TO THE OCEAN

OCEAN

An Ocean is a very huge body covered of salt water. It presents 70% of Earth's surface. There is only one world ocean, it is divided into five main areas with no borders. Smaller parts of the ocean are called seas.

PACIFIC

Pacific Ocean is the largest of Earth's oceans. Its surface is more than all the dry lands together. It is bounded by the continents of Asia and Australia in the west and the Americas in the east.

ATLANTIC

Atlantic Ocean is the second largest of Earth's oceans. Most of Earth rivers water flow into the Atlantic. Its S-shaped basin extending longitudinally between Europe and Africa to the east, and the Americas to the west

INDIAN

Indian Ocean is the third largest of Earth's oceans. It was sailed by traders to exchange goods between India, Africa, and Arabia. It is bounded by Asia to the north, Africa to the west and Australia to the east

ARCTIC

Arctic Ocean is the world smallest and shallowest ocean. It is also known by being the coldest. than all the dry lands together. It occupies the most northern region of Earth.

SOUTHERN

The Southern Ocean is also known as the Antarctic Ocean because it surrounds Antarctica.

OCEAN MOST WONDERFUL ANIMALS

My Name Is CRAB

CRAB

I am decapod, which means I am ten-footed. I live in all the world's oceans, in fresh water, and on land. There are over 4500 species of me.

My Name Is SHARK

SHARK

I don't have any bone in my body.
I live for about 25 years.
You might know me as human-killer
but I only attack if I am scared.

OCTOPUS

I have three hearts.
I have very good eyesight and an excellent sense of touch.
I am invertebrate, which means I have no backbones.

My Name Is STARFISH

STARFISH

I can only live in warm water.
I am invertebrate too.
I have five arms.
Unlike you, I don't have blood.

My Name Is OYSTER

OYSTER

I am edible. I like to eat algae, which is a type of plant material that lives in the water. I have shells that are usually shaped like ovals or pears

My Name Is DOLPHIN

DOLPHIN

I am a marine mammal.
I breathe through a blowhole on the top of my head.
I am carnivore, I eat mostly fish and squid. I'm the most intelligent animal in the ocean.

My

Name

Is

SEA TURTLE

SEA TURTLE

I can hold my breath for 30 minutes. I can't live on the Arctic Ocean because it's too cold there. I eat all kinds of food including sea grass, seaweed, crabs, jellyfish, and shrimp

My Name Is SEAL

SEAL

I am carnivorous mammal.
I usually feeds on fish,
squid, shellfish, crustaceans
or sea birds.
i can sleep underwater.

SEA HORSE

I am a tiny fis. They call me Sea horse cause my head looks like a tiny horse.
I am carnivore too.

www.ingramcontent.com/pod-product-compliance
Lightning Source LLC
Chambersburg PA
CBHW081629100526
44590CB00021B/3670